Earth Loyalty and Bioregional Practice

Earth Loyalty & Bioregional Practice

Selected Writings

FREDERICK R. CERVIN

New Haven Bioregional Publications

New Haven, Connecticut

New Haven-Quinnipiac
Bioregional Group

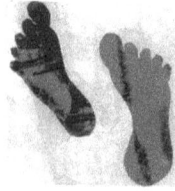

Leaving a Small Footprint

New Haven Bioregional Publications
New Haven, Connecticut

Copyright © 2015 New Haven–Quinnipiac Bioregional Group

ISBN: 978-0-9908460-0-0
Library of Congress Control Number: 2014956511

Printed in the United States of America

p 10 9 8 7 6 5 4 3 2 1

PROJECT EDITING
Maria Tupper
Mark Mitsock
Aaron Goode

MANUSCRIPT EDITING
Anne Cherry

BOOK DESIGN
AND TYPOGRAPHY
William Meyers

COVER DESIGN
AND ART
Domingo Medina

For Maria
whose gardening is good for the soul

Contents

Preface

FRED CERVIN believed that the relation of the human species to the natural world is in a state of crisis, and that this crisis has both a practical and a spiritual dimension. The pragmatic and the spiritual are typically thought to operate on separate planes, but in Fred's vision they are seamlessly blended, as expressed in the poetry and prose gathered in this volume.

Fred's writings explore a common set of themes from different angles. Two central themes are modern man's faith in technological progress and the ecological catastrophe this leads us toward. Progress has become the religion of modern humanity, the faith of our times, and Fred dissects the spiritual and ecological impact of this faith. The technological revolution has given us great material wealth as a species, yet, ironically, life for most individuals has become less satisfying, because we live in social systems that cut us off from our roots in local communities and the earth. The constant growth that is the hallmark of technological society is inconsistent with the inescapable laws of ecology that govern all life on earth. As we deplete earth's supply of fossil fuels, humanity is heading toward a cliff at an ever-accelerating pace. Even if the human species can somehow avoid this calamity, it is already a reality for the other species with which we share the planet; a holocaust of the earth has already taken place.

How do we turn this situation around? Answering this question provides Fred with another set of themes: bioregionalism, the generative community, and Earth Loyalty. Bioregionalism is a practical way for human communities to reconnect to the earth and their local environments. The current era of high-energy lifestyles inevitably must come to an end; living locally will once again become a necessity. By adopting bioregional practices, we can begin preparing for this transition now. In the process, we will find that we have come across a more satisfying lifestyle.

In envisioning this transition, Fred explores the creativity that comes from small face-to-face groups, the "generative community." The top-down, command-and-control model of social organization that came with industrialism and the megalopolis needs to be replaced with small, creative, self-organizing social units.

But breaking the hold that faith in endless growth and progress currently has on humanity will require a radical change in spiritual orientation, akin to a religious conversion. Fred called this new spiritual orientation Earth Loyalty, and it is the central idea around which all Fred's other ideas revolve. We must switch our loyalty from technology and economic growth to the earth as the true source of all goods, literally the ground of our being. This is the way forward.

—*Mark Mitsock*
New Haven, Connecticut
January 2015

Earth Loyalty and Bioregional Practice

Three Medicine Songs

I

Sinking down into the soft earth
The worms caress my body
The black mould opens to receive me
Closes gently over my white nakedness

The earth is warm
Even the worms are warm
Their bodies filled with light
Exuding a slippery liquid
They slide over my flesh
Hundreds of them
Moved by great love

Tears of gratitude
Seep from my sleeping eyes

II

A voice cries:
Homage to the hag!
I bow and kiss the earth before her
I forsake my arrogant plan
to build the Ideal City

She is merciful
She raises me up
She embraces my only anguished
Dying life in the great
Anguished dying life of
All things

Tears stream from my eyes
As I see in her ugly hag face
Sublime beauty

I am received into the
Womb of Time

III

After long busyness I have come
Into the quiet beating of
My own heart

A lifetime spent within
Right angles and
Right thoughts and even
At times
Right actions
Has not changed this
Rhythmic drawing in and
Pushing out

Like a lordly lion my heart goes on
Through all weather
Or like a seal
Soaring
In the depths of the Sea

I do not cause my heart to beat
Or determine its force
And speed.

How wonderful to feel
This sweet wild life
Here
Inside my chest.

———————————————

1984

After a Poem of Rilke

Ruthlessly torn
from the Mother's body,
chipped out with picks and shovels,
blasted with dynamite,
chewed away
by immense steel teeth,
the ore flows to the mills
and the furnaces —
at first on the backs
of conscripted peasants and mules,
later on broad conveyor belts
and in railroad cars.

The ore is crushed.
The metal driven from it
by intense heat
pours into moulds,
assumes the alien form
of the moulds.

The metal so separated and refined
moves out from the smelting places
to factories and workshops
where human beings made unnaturally rational
by injections of knowledge
shape it into useful objects,
or any objects
that will sell.

People buy it
use it
hoard it
lose it
throw it away.

The metal is filled
with yearning.

Derelict cars
in the dooryards of Maine,
abandoned railroad tracks,
children's toys,
wrenches lost and rusting
in the grass,
battleships lying in the canyons of the sea—
stir restlessly.

They long to be home again
deep in the living rock.

The great steel girders
that hold up Manhattan,
bright new fuel-efficient cars
just off the ship from Japan,

copper-bottomed kettles
on the shelves of hardware stores,
bomb casings
and the hulls of rockets,
ingots of gold in Fort Knox—
they too feel the magnetism.

All the metal in the world
"wants to go back into the veins
of the thrown-open mountain,
which will close again behind it."

All the metal in the world
dreams—

> *Deep in the Mother's body*
> *it will absorb energy.*
> *Transfused with the plasma*
> *of the Mother*
> *it will glow with the ardor*
> *of its own original being.*

> *Pulses of light*
> *rhythmically shake*
> *the whole interior*
> *of the Mother's body.*

1988

The Earth Is Enough

Wandering long without a home
So high above it all
We never knew our living place
Never found our people.

Now we're starting to come to
Knowing our relations
Moving on a downward way
Approaching our beloved.

How solid is this earth we walk
How real is this body!
All we hunger for is here
No need to fly up yonder.

Every living thing is kin
To us the human beings.
And in this mortal company
We find our true fulfillment.

Sung to the tune "I know where I'm going."

Evil gamblers roll the dice
Without remorse or feeling
But we resist their empire
Defending our beloved.

Laying waste the mighty trees
Poisoning the oceans
They do not recognize the ones
Who gave them life and succor.

In awe and deep complicity
We drink from ceaseless fountains!
The earth it is enough!
We long for nothing other.

Death it is no enemy
But peaceful consummation
For those who drank their fill in life
Of earth's dark wondrous body.

1999

Fantasia for the Fourth of July

It is time.
Say *independence*, then.
Say *liberty*.

It is time for the rats in the sewers to
    strike for freedom.
Time for the cancer cells, wild with desire,
    to proliferate inside the comatose body.
Time for the dancers to invent new dances
    to a music of unknown provenance.
Time for the drifters to drift, picking
    up new lovers as they go.
Time for molecules to vibrate more intensely.
Time for the earth herself to quake in jubilation
    shaking off the old lessons of the masters like a
    cow shaking off flies.
It is time for Africa now.
Time for the African rhythms so long familiar to our ears
    to penetrate all the way in.
Time for infectious madness to possess us completely.

Time for our own black desires to come
   out of the closet:

The desire to open all the windows and all the doors.
The desire to bathe naked in the surging sea.
The desire to become trees.
The desire to kiss the earth.
The desire to eat dirt.
The desire to eat insects.
The desire to couple with animals.
The desire to know even as we also are known.

The desire to take to the open road, exploring without
   limit the question: *What does desire want?*

Do you think you know the answer?
Only the dancers know.
Dare to know then!
Let the feet declare their independence
   running as they will
   dancing as they will
   the slow dance of new lovers who
   touch the earth with tears and
   on to the frenzied dance of
   full communion.

Declare liberty throughout the land, unto
   all the inhabitants thereof!
Let the drummers be free to drum
   the potters to pot
   the dreamers to dream
   the singers to sing
   the talkers to talk
   the thinkers to think!

Let the wings be free to beat at last
    the roots to plunge
    the bacteria to swarm (they already are)
    the teeth to crunch
    the intestines to digest
    the genitals to swish
    the brains to glow
    the uteruses to contract!

Let the reins go slack!
Let the horse run for the sheer joy of it!
Let the energies of life declare their independence.
Let each cell express its intelligence.
Let every fiber of existence have a mind of its own.
Let viroid life invade the media of domination.
Let love's excess fabricate the new communities.
Let the outcast and forgotten climb up onto
    the soapbox.

Trust the earth!
Every heart vibrates to that iron string!

Open the gates of the dungeon!
Blow trumpets, ring bells, beat drums!
She it is, Queen under the hill!
She comes forth dancing and rattling
    her castanets
    like an army terrible with banners!

It is the earth now declares her independence
    with wild laughter in her eyes!

Dare to embrace her!
Dare drink from her foaming cup!

---

4 JULY 2003

riverrun

all passes
nothing remains
said Heraclitus

to accept
this saying
as a blessing
not a curse

is my
religion

---

21 AUGUST 2004

That-Which-Flows Sent Me

Empire is about dams —
about blocking, impounding,
diverting and redirecting
flows
of water, of energy, of raw materials,
of thought, of desire, of feeling.

Empire is about controlling
and harnessing
the flowing life of the world.

It is about making money flow uphill
through the deployment of skillful,
cunning, devious means.
All roads must converge in
Grand Central Terminal.
All cars must run on rigid rails
laid down in perfect order
in this best of all possible worlds,
this Empire of manufactured objects.

But all that which flows
has a will and a mind
of its own.
All that which flows
is alive with power
from within itself.

Empire is obliged to beg, borrow
or steal its power from the only source
there is, namely
That-Which-Flows.

That-Which-Flows is alive with
its own life.
It borrows not,
begs not,
steals not.
Alive with its own life,
its own juice,
it flows on.
If it encounters a block

it simply builds up until it
overflows the barrier.

All blocks and dams are temporary.
That-Which-Flows outlasts them all.

Empires collapse.
That-Which-Flows
will never cease.

You can poison the sexuality of the masses
with guilt and shame, but

you cannot shut it down.
You can ban the use of drums
but the slaves will beat out rhythms
on their own bodies.
They will create work songs
which provide new channels
for the driving power of the drum,
the same complex rhythms
as before.
They will innocently sing these
rhythmic songs in the
very teeth
of the overseers.

The Empire of Mass Consumption
skillfully, craftily
dams, impounds, diverts and controls
That-Which-Flows in us.
The energies of life,
the desires of this body,
it tames and disciplines, causing them
to flow into the malls,
into the cars,
into the clothes and makeup,
into the entertainment carefully designed to serve
the purposes of the Masters.

The flows of thought and feeling,
the blood which is our life,
they seduce to flow through the turbines of
corporate power.
Private syndicates generate enormous profits
from a system of locks and dams

and canals of feeling,
a system of pipes and valves
so complicated that we don't even know
what is happening to us.

We are led to the slaughter
by our own desire.

But I tell you now —
Understand this!
A change is coming.
The Empire is in big trouble.
The flow of Oil from
impoverished desert kingdoms
begins to fail.

Those at the top
can scarcely conceal
their panic.
Arrogant braggadocio
reveals desperation
not strength.

Twenty-five empires
known to history
have collapsed
due to ecological
overdrafts.
The present and first ever
world-wide empire
will soon follow suit.

All human beings everywhere
will suffer the effects
of this disaster.

That-Which-Flows
will not miss a beat.

This is the moment
of dangerous opportunity,
a chance for real adventures
and novel experiments.

That-Which-Flows
will break through the dikes.
Valves of the heart
long closed up like stone
will open.
The Water of Life
will seek new paths
out of its own surpassing abundance.

People will open up new
channels of two-way communication.
They will establish new connections.
Romeo will marry Juliet
against imperial law and custom.
In the absence of TV sedatives
human beings will invent new pleasures,
dance new dances,
open up new territories.

That-Which-Flows
makes no distinction
between the festival of death
and the festival of life.
The corpses of a defeated army
are the feast of crows,
vultures and coyotes.

Desire makes its own way
in the world.
New life wells up from deep underground
in the craters of catastrophe.

As the soft flowing
water of the great river
creates the Grand Canyon,
so That-Which-Flows
erodes the power of
the powers-that-be, opens up
new channels, and creates
fantastic forms,
stunning works of art
out of the ruins of
thrones and dominions.

Here then is what you must do:
Unplug from established channels.
Make new connections.

Taste forbidden pleasures.
Make of your life an adventure,
a series of experiments.
Dare to explore
those possibilities formerly
blanked out by the Wizard's
Grandiose Spectacle.
Court new experiences.
Reach out and touch
those persons formerly
forbidden to you.
Dive deep into the flowing rivers
of the earth.

Abandon yourself to the dance.
Commune utterly with
That-Which-Flows.
Invent new forms of life.
Do not wait for instructions
from those higher up.
You are the ones —
the people we've all been waiting for —
strong enough to love
this fate prepared for you by
the chances of time.
Without resentment or remorse,
give yourselves up to the secret currents of
Irresistible Life.

---

22 APRIL 2005

Bioregional Activity

BIOREGIONAL ACTIVITY IS a way of seeking to restore our lost connection with the earth. It differs from other ways in its recognition that connection requires specific points of contact. Seeking awareness of the earth in our own locale, we walk over the land knowing with our feet, our bodies, the reality of her body — which is still there, still present under the spectacular veneer with which modern society has covered it. Even when we have rearranged physical features and water flows; even when we have utterly destroyed the life communities which covered a region only a century or two ago, the earth is still present. It is still possible to know her, to hear her breathing, to feel her life.

Bioregional practice, even when it is most mundane, is spiritual practice — because it enhances our awareness at the roots of our being of the nourishing source upon which we depend. It establishes new flows of energy, new filaments of ecological participation, between our re-inhabitory human group and the earth — which receives and bears our whole weight and impact at every moment, here, in this place. Everything we do and are is already a part of her rich flowing life. Bioregional activity is becoming conscious of this reality. Bioregional practice is an expression of our commitment to the earth not in a general way, not focused on far-off regions, but in the concreteness and specificity and here-ness of everyday life.

Bioregional activity is like marriage: it is not always romantic, but it is always real. We have decided to be married to our own life-place. This commitment requires of us an ongoing revision and renewal of our priorities and way of life. It requires us to form new relationships with the people of our area as well as with the other living beings who dwell in this place. It requires us to participate in the decision-making processes that affect the people, the lands, the watercourses, the plants and the animals of our area. As in marriage each spouse acts out a loving commitment in the details of everyday activity, so we act out our love and deep commitment to this place. We might have lived elsewhere, might have married otherwise. But we didn't. We came somehow to this specific place, and that has made all the difference. Beginning from where we are, we discover a wonderful new meaning in our lives. No doubt it was always there — at least as a possibility — but now we embrace it consciously and with due deliberation. Now we are married. Now we know where we stand. Slowly we discover how to live, what to do. Our new relationship with our place is the source of this new wisdom. It is all so simple, so concrete, not at all abstruse.

Bioregional activity is the way to a new blessing of our lives here and now, in this body, on this earth, in this place. It is the basis for a new community. We the lost, we the displaced, we the uprooted, we the alienated — products as we are of a tumultuous, ever-advancing modernity — have a chance to find home again. This commitment does not set us at odds with people who live elsewhere. Far from it! We are spiritually akin to all those who lovingly care for their own places, everywhere. All together, caring for our own life-places and resisting those who would despoil us, we come into a new hope for humanity as a whole, for the future of the earth. Humbly taking up the tasks of caring for the earth in our own place, we join hands with people everywhere who are making a similar commitment.

Bioregional activity is the metabolism of a new civilization, a new era of human life on earth. Breathing deeply, grounded in our own life-place, we will find the strength we need to resist tyranny. We have been in the grip of a placeless, earth-devouring monster. Now we are drawing the line: We will deny the ravager access to the life of our place. No longer will we turn over, without a qualm, the life of our own lands to those who live elsewhere — those who care nothing for us or our region and for whom we and our place are merely means to their ends. In the name of the earth we resist this domination, and call upon people everywhere to join us in a similar resistance in their own living places. We decline to play this game any longer.

It is time to put the nipples back on the goddess.

JULY 2005

Lose Your Faith!

(A Little Sermon about Progress)

THE UTOPIA OF modern times was based on a vision of *control through knowledge*. Human good was to be achieved through domination of nature. "We must put nature on the rack and extract her secrets from her," wrote Francis Bacon early in the seventeenth century. Through the new sciences we shall become "the masters and possessors of nature," promised René Descartes at around the same time.

Women too had to be subjected and controlled, their sexuality and emotional energies taken out of action. This was the era of witch persecution when women were forced to undergo judicial torture, being stretched on the rack in order to extract from them confessions of foul intercourse with the devil and knowledge of infernal workings. Bacon was a lawyer and had experience. He knew what he was talking about. The metaphor of "putting nature on the rack" came easily to his mind. The modern utopia was misogynistic from the get-go. The power and influence which at least some women enjoyed during the Renaissance was slowly whittled away during the ensuing centuries.

Gradually all remnants of the feminine and/or the erotic were stripped away from the Main Program. In the Middle Ages knowledge had been embedded in everyday practices, and the highest knowledge—of God and divine things—was impossible to attain unless reason were aided by heavenly grace. The state of the knower's soul was not a matter of indifference as it later became. Only in our greatly admired era of Progress did knowledge become inherently cold-blooded and "value-neutral." Puritanical suppression of erotic love freed vast emotional energies which could be invested in the comforts and elegances of civilization, and in empire building. Denial of the body created huge reservoirs of hate, which could be mobilized in the endless wars of modernity.

Auschwitz and Hiroshima revealed just how value-neutral the priests of pure knowledge had become. Bacon had already spelled out the secret code of Progress long before, but these horrific events of the twentieth century revealed it openly: control through knowledge. Reason alone without love or prejudice would carry the Program through all the way to the end: the complete, radical rationalization of everything. We are talking here about a linear, one-dimensional, mechanical way of thinking. Knowledge has been reduced to pure, neutral information. All prejudice and bias have been excised from the hearts of the master knowers, including the prejudice in favor of humanity, the bias in favor of life, the irrational love of children. And love of the earth? *Fuhgeddaboudit!* Knowledge, *knowledge über alles*: this was the secret code. And, through knowledge, total control. In the past it was understood that knowledge and love must be linked in the superior person; this was the ideal of wisdom, an ideal now relegated to greeting-card sentimentality. In practice wisdom has no operational function in modern times. It is excluded. Only value-neutral knowledge gets any respect.

After the collapse of the Soviet Union, George H. W. Bush announced the arrival of the New World Order. Even at the time the phrase seemed to have a cold, uncanny flavor: shades of the Thousand Year Reich. The New World Order is the final stage of Progress: the Control Society.

Nowadays misogynistic images of women flood the media. Nuclear weapons proliferate along with increasingly urgent advocacy of their use. After all, "Why have this beautiful military if you can't use it?" as the first female U.S. Secretary of State so aptly put it. If you have the ultimate tool of total control, you're going to use it, no?

Indeed, we have been waging a sort of stealth nuclear war for many years now, first in Yugoslavia, then in Afghanistan, and in Iraq. We have sown their fields with depleted uranium, yielding already a rich harvest of birth defects, cancers and mental breakdowns. Universal surveillance has been imposed here at home. Torture has now been accepted as just one more necessary tool in our already bulging toolkit, as we move on to the absolute utopia: *Full-Spectrum Dominance.* In order to control nature, it turns out, you have to control people as well— which for most of us means we have to accept *being controlled.*

This is the package which has been sold to us.

We have achieved the utopia of Bacon and Descartes. It is utter devastation and disaster. It can and will get a lot worse if we keep going the way we are going. Our culture has objectified nature. It has objectified colonized peoples. It has objectified women. It has objectified the various sorts of *Untermenschen* here at home. And there is no place whatsoever for earth-based peoples in the ideal city of our modern dream. We are turning many of our young men into Rambo robots, addicted to pornography and incapable of real relationship. Finally, all of us who identify with the Masters and their program objectify our own souls. We employ every sort of drug and psycho-technology in order to adjust our inmost being to the Program. You are either for the Program or against the Program. Mostly we are poor weak people . . . we want to be on the side of the winners. We want to be safe.

But wait. . . . A doubt appears in spite of universal propaganda. . . . What if those who are presently riding high . . . what if they are not the winners after all? What if the days of the Total Control Society are numbered? It is getting harder and harder to conceal the fact that we are turning the earth into a desert. This is supposed to be some kind of success for the Lords of Progress? What if, during an unmedicated moment, a feeling of disgust for the Program rises from your deep insides? We are coming into the End-game of the Modern Utopia. The oceans are dying. The Amazon rain forest, according to one current theory, might suddenly flip, becoming a dry desert within a period of only two or three years. We hope this isn't true. And the ice is melting, no doubt about it. These are facts.

We must turn away from this vision of Control through Knowledge. We must admit to ourselves that the cold-blooded, objective approach hasn't worked out as promised. It's time for the reign of the lizard-men to end. *It is time to lose our faith in Progress.* I am talking about a radical existential crisis. Like the coyote in the Road Runner cartoon, we suddenly look down and realize that there is no ground underneath our feet. Our whole culture has been living a fantasy. Loss of faith means: you just don't believe in it anymore. It is not going to work out. Our present state of disconnection from the earth, from the community of living beings, from our own bodies, and from each other . . . is *suicidal.* Civilization has become a suicide pact: this is what will be revealed to you when you lose your faith in Progress.

To lose one's religion can be a shattering experience. Survival is not guaranteed. You need something to fill the void. But your chances of making it will probably be pretty good if you find a new, more adequate object for your affections, your trust, and your ultimate loyalty. Progress has been at the center of our identity. Our teachers taught us this. But now we have reached the breaking point and we need new loyalties, new watchwords, a new vision:

> *The earth is enough.*
> *Women and men together, learning the path by walking it.*
> *Love the earth!*
> *Earthly love is best.*
> *Stay put!*

Get married to a particular place. Dwell there. Learn to know and love the Earth through an ongoing, intimate relationship, an attachment to a place. To understand the beloved is to love her more, and to love her better. The institutions of knowledge and science must undergo a profound metamorphosis. Instead of control and domination, science must aim at knowing the Earth in order to preserve and fulfill her, and in order to accommodate our human lifeways to her nature.

> *We, not the earth, must yield and adjust.*
> *She must increase. We must decrease.*

No doubt this idea seems extreme and utopian, but it is no more utopian than the modern program was at its inception. And it is the only path which offers us a way out of the trap which the world has become. We must rejoin the Community of Life. We must confess that the Laws of Ecology apply to humans just as much as to other species. The workings of the modern machine are well known to us. Nothing but further devastation awaits us if we allow this dystopian machine of Progress to continue to grind up the world.

It's a dead end, folks. We know this in our hearts, but we don't want to admit it. We don't want to admit that we invested all that we had in a failure. We don't want to give up our faith in this god which has failed us. We don't know who we will be . . . if we lose this faith that has so totally defined us and made us who we are.

It is time for us to repent now. Our sin is this: We have failed the earth. We have not loved her as we ought to have done. *Utilitarianism cannot grasp this.* And she says to us: OK. One last chance: *This time, don't fail me!*

It is a great grief to admit that we have despoiled and raped and wrecked our own Mother. It is a horror to allow ourselves to feel how cold and empty and hopeless this artificial world of Progress has become. *How meaningless our improved gadgets are on a burned-out planet!*

Turn your hearts away, then, from the arrogant cruelty of the New World Order. Renounce the cold-blooded god of Progress and all his violent ways. Put away the satisfactions of flying high and fast above a smoking and pillaged earth. Repent of your desire to build the Ideal City on the ruined and shattered body of your own Mother.

Love the earth. Turn now to her with all your heart. She is the one who has given us everything. Relax into this reality. We can never be grateful enough to her. And after all our terrifying mistakes, she is still giving to us. We are still utterly dependent upon her. Let us attach ourselves to her as a baby holds to its mother's breast. Let us love her also with a mature love, an adult love, a deeply fulfilling love.

Making love with her, face-to-face.

Friends, consider it: *Why else do we live?*

SEPTEMBER 2007

Crying for a Vision

On Becoming a Generative Community

It doth not yet appear what we shall be. Can we become self-organizing, as nature is?

Instead of a flock of sheep, directed from outside by a shepherd or dog, a pack of wolves.

Instead of a hierarchical state or corporation or army, a tribe.

Instead of a king or president in whom power is focused, chiefs. Special chiefs for special purposes. The war chief: for each war a different chief. The farm chief. The art chief. The science chief. The dancing chief. The music chief. The cooking chief. The funeral chief.

Always subject to recall at any time. The chief is extruded by the pack, spontaneously. The tribe organizes itself by a kind of Brownian motion.

The tribe, or the pack, moves freely over the smooth open space of the plateau. It resists being incorporated into any sort of state or empire.

The earth, the universe as a whole, produces order from below by the spontaneous interactions of living particles. Species arise out of the processes of time, products not of the workshop with its plans and blueprints but rather of the interactions of desiring particles, each going about its own business.

What we might become is a community which lives along the lines of nature's flows. We could become an expression of self-organizing life. We could relate to each other, and to the world around us, as a swarm of bees or a pack of wolves. No regimentation. An individual wolf might be now at the center of the pack, now at the periphery. She acts always for herself, always alone; yet at the same time her moves are always synchronized with the fluid movements of the pack. A great flock of birds wheels across the sky; no one bird bumps into another one. A flock of starlings, or perhaps better, of crows. A little ungainly, perhaps a little clumsy at times, yet still they are a flock, still they move together toward wherever they must go. If there is a leader, we can't tell which one it is.

We could embody by conscious intent in our life together the ecological order of the earth, the interconnectedness of all things.

Each wolf is a co-creator of the pack. The health and well-being of the pack is the health and well-being of the individual wolf. The health and well-being of the individual wolf is the health and well-being of the pack. The intelligence, the vision, the cunning of the pack *as a whole* emerges spontaneously from all the members living straight ahead, following the path of desire.

"Follow your bliss."

We might embody in our life *as a human community* the same principles which are operative in the entire community of all life. We could reject the idea of conquering nature. We could give up the notion that instinct/desire is the enemy. Instead of being the dam, we could be the river flowing free.

A complex, many-dimensional life together. Each of us a complex, many-dimensional person.

A gang of fools, drunk on the energies of life. Participants in the wild, lively creativity which is inherent in this earth on which we dwell.

True life is not elsewhere. True life is here. The spirit is poured out on the whole community. Each particle is charged with life and power. Every project is another throw of the dice in the great game. We have no wish to found an empire, nor to be an ideological support of imperial domination. We do not desire to organize our area into a territory unified from above by an orthodox creed to which all must consent. A creed like "Shop till you drop," for example.

We don't want conformity — far from it! We revel in the diversity and strangeness of life. Sometimes grotesque, but always beautiful.

We seek allies in the great game. At stake is the future of our species on this earth. We learn how to live at peace with nature. We take dancing lessons, learning the cool moves of those who are well adapted to their place. Living on the earth, living well on the earth as full participants, finding satisfaction not in destroying the web of life but in delicate and appropriate interactions with all other living beings around us.

When the hive gets too large, the worker bees feed one of the larvae on special food so that it grows into a new queen. The new queen flies away, taking half of the hive with her, and establishes a new community elsewhere. There is no general headquarters of the bees of Turtle Island. There is no national government of the bees. Each hive is independent, yet they multiply.

Viral transmission. All we have to do is become fully alive, praising and affirming in all that we do the amazing wild life that moves through all things. As we find joy ourselves, as we are whirled up in the dance ourselves, participating in the intensity of the life of the pack in its locale, alive with the greater life, we will touch the lives of others. Viral transmission will occur. Contact will be made.

When you fall in love, people notice something is different in you. "Exuberance is beauty," said Blake. We will find our people. Many will turn away, afraid to become disturbingly alive. But some will be infected. Some will say, "I want to become a part of this, whatever it is. I want to belong to this self-organizing pack, where they are all following their bliss wherever it leads."

The times require a new vision. The present dominant belief system is on a collision course with realities that cannot be pushed aside any longer. Inventing liberties as we go, we have got to work out the complex fabric of a whole new nature-friendly culture. Need I add that it will be friendly to *human nature* at the deepest level, as well as to nature in general? William James said that the great eras of human history all have this in common, that people rediscovered a profound correspondence, an appropriateness, a fit, between their own human being and the being of the world around them. Reality affords us that which we most deeply require. We can be at home in the universe. There is no separation. This is the vision the world of our time needs desperately. This is the way out of the trap which the world has become. We can become a part of a People to Come, a People of the Future, who will be comfortable in an ever-shifting complex world of multiple flows. Their faith will be in the processes of time and change, not in a supposedly stable, rocklike Absolute, outside of time.

SEPTEMBER 2008

Earth Loyalty
As a Spiritual Orientation[2]/
Queen of My Heart

I can hear the Earth Goddess breathing.
She is near.
She is at hand.
She is not far away.
She is as close as my own breathing body,
as near as the beating of my heart,
as intimate to me as the air in my lungs,
as present as the weather, or the sea's caress.

Can you find it in your heart to love Her?
Can you find it in your soul to have a care for Her,
for the Earth that has given us everything?

Forgive me, Mama.
They were beating You, and I turned away.
They were raping You, and I averted my eyes.
They were sucking You dry as they partied on,
and I joined in, although I was
ashamed to do so.

[2] Sermon preached to the First Unitarian Universalist Society of New Haven, May 10, 2009

• • •

We are confronting these days a great triple crisis: oil depletion, climate change and money meltdown. I believe that the most important thing we can do in response to this is to

> *Take the vow of Earth Loyalty*
> and then share this decision
> this profound change
> with others.
> Instead of a "decision for Christ,"
> what we need today is
> *a decision for the earth.*

Make your vow to the earth! Promise to live in your place with love, consideration, and respect. Withdraw your trust from stupid giants, organizations so large that they cannot function without damaging surrounding life and structures.

Recognize that the earth gave us life. The earth and the sun sustain us in life. Say no to the magic of the factories that transform earth's forms into junk within at most ten years. Say no to care-less manipulation as the Source of Human Good. Say yes to the wisdom that says knowledge without love is a blind, power-hungry dictator, a cold-blooded monster. The head cannot rule over the heart without producing apocalyptic destruction.

Love the earth! is the only way left now, the only way out of the trap which the world has become. Unless we love the earth, we will not survive. Our species will disappear not because we cannot do the math but because of a failure to love. We will disappear because we have banished the poets from the public square. There is no hope for us as long as we do not acknowledge our error.

I vow to love the earth. I vow to meditate day and night on the meaning of this new love which I have found, this new passion for the earth which illuminates my path as I live on into the future we lovers will create together.

I say no to a purely utilitarian relationship with the earth. I will not engage in "value-neutral" discussion with those who repudiate *Love the earth!*

as a romantic daydream. *I say no* to the gangsters of doom who continue the insane project of modernity: "We shall be the Masters and Possessors of Nature." They have put my Mother on the rack; they are raping my beloved. They delight in their illusory triumph over her.

I vow to love the earth with my whole heart, soul, mind, and strength.

We must give up flying, not only because of its large contribution to global warming, but perhaps more importantly because of its power as a religious ceremony. "Up! Up! And away!" Flying expresses and reinforces our assumed role as masters of the earth. It is a prime expression of our feeling of entitlement. At thirty thousand feet above the ground we lose all perspective on where we fit in to the ecological order, the life communities of the earth. All our aspirations to go higher, to "slip the surly bonds of earth," find their fulfillment in a 747. Flying is the physical expression of our delusions of grandeur, our elation, our inflated sense of our right to rule. To go on to the stars, to master not only the earth but also the universe, is the next step. Those who love the earth will renounce flying because it is the arch-ritual of Man-the-Master. Man the Counter-Creator. *Menschen, Menschen über Alles!*

• • •

No. I vow loyalty to the earth. I vow to love the earth. I vow to remain connected to the earth all the days of my life. I aspire to be on the journey downward, not the way of starry supremacy. I aspire to be at home on earth, as the animals are, not to fly as angels above.

What we need now, more than anything, is a ritual of refusal and of affirmation. By refusing to fly, we deliberately offend the modern sensibility which finds human domination utterly natural and appropriate. By refusing to fly, we affirm our contentment with having our feet here on earth. By abandoning all dreams of some "better place," we confess how much we love the earth.

There is still time to avoid the worst of global warming, but in order to do so, we need an immediate shutdown, which cannot come about through rational arguments. Some other extremely effective factor must come into play in order to create a phase change. The only model available is sudden, drastic religious conversion, similar to the evangelical awakenings of American history or to the spread of Islam from Spain to India in less than a century.

In a terrifying vacuum of meaning, a culture in free fall as the future reality of life on earth sinks in to our deeper minds, people will be ready to grab onto anything that promises an anchor, a new center of stability, in a world spinning out of control. Earth Loyalty, *Love the earth!* is this new center. This needs to be available to people as an alternative way of organizing their lives and culture—now, while the forces of disintegration fly around us like a snowstorm.

• • •

We have no regard for the earth. It is of no account in our calculations and strategies. We approach the earth with an attitude of depraved indifference.

Rising population shows our species narcissism. The birth rate in the US reached its all-time-highest level in 2007. What is humanism? Is it not a continuation of theism by other means after the Death of God? We live in a bubble of our own self-importance. By contrast, an earth-centered spirituality would recognize that humans stand in a subsidiary, dependent position in relation to the earth. The earth is a Sacred Goddess, and we have sinned against her. Sinned grievously.

I hold that the first principle of religion in our time is, *Love the earth!* To see earth as but a pile of raw materials awaiting transformation into human artifacts, is false religion, the religion of Man-As-God. The Christian fundamentalists are correct in believing that man is not God. They are deluded in their idea that the whole universe exists as but a stage on which the history and destiny of man-with-God is being played out.

Man is not the center. For humans today the earth is central. Only by recognizing the earth as the Source of Human Good will humans find that spiritual orientation which they will need if they are to survive during the era of the Death of Man, the era which comes after the era of the Death of God. "Man" cannot take the place of the missing God. Only the earth can, the earth understood as the incarnation of cosmic life and creativity in our local part of the universe. The creative power of the universe declares itself in the whole fabric of life on earth.

Once we set out on the path of earth conquest, we were marching toward our own doom. Subduing the earth has resulted in the destruction of the earth as a suitable habitat for humans. If we want to survive, we will have to get used to the idea that we must submit to the earth, i.e, to the laws of ecology. There is no other way. There are laws on this earth, and we will either live by them or go the way of all flesh before our time.

• • •

I would like you to make your decision for Mother Earth now — *today*.

You shall say:

Forgive me, Mama, for I have forgotten you. I have had no regard for you, even though I knew that all my life depends on your greater life.

Therefore I commit myself to have a care for you in all that I do.

I will have no more than one child during my lifetime.

I will never fly in an airplane.

I will move toward subsistence, producing for myself a part of what I need to live; and I will move away from consumerism, a lifestyle based on buying everything I need, a lifestyle of abject dependence on huge systems over which I can have minimal influence.

I will reduce my consumption of meat to a minimum.

I will progressively reduce my use of my car until ultimately I will no longer own a car at all.

I will not watch TV more than one hour per week.

I will buy local whenever possible. I will get all my food within a fifty-mile radius.

I will never speak disparagingly or cynically of the earth, or of the community of living beings, or of the human body, or of the genitals which give us life.

Every day I will mourn the destruction of nature in our time. Every day I will pray to Mother Earth to ask forgiveness for my participation in this damage, a participation that I may hope to reduce but cannot avoid altogether as a member of modern society.

The decision I am making today is open-ended; I will understand it better by and by, and will refine my practices accordingly.

I will refuse employment in industries that are notorious earth destroyers. If need be, I will accept a life of poverty before I will rape and batter my own mother.

I vow this day loyalty to the earth above all else. I will love the earth here in my own place, where I am practically connected and grounded in the great living planet. I renounce all other or former loyalties, except insofar as they are compatible with this vow I am taking today.

I will love the earth with my whole heart, soul, mind and strength.

• • •

Unless we personify Earth, we will not be able to repent, will not change enough, or soon enough. The writing is on the wall, stark and terrible. Implacable forces are already in play. The future of our species on this planet is at stake. It's not just at risk. Don't say it's *at risk*. Disaster is a *certainty* if we don't change *radically*. We are on a runaway train heading toward an abyss.

All this is happening because we have forgotten our Mother the Earth. We have no regard for her. We make our most consequential economic decisions without a thought for Earth. We treat her like an inert mass of raw materials or like a sterile desert of no use except as a place to throw our garbage. What we have lost fundamentally is a fresh, lively sense of our own dependence. We think of our relations with Earth as environmentalism—as if Earth were a mere externality, something in need of minimal maintenance—rather than being bone of our bone and flesh of our flesh. "Mother Nature" is a tired, worn-out figure of speech, useful only for sentimental greeting cards. The reality is quite different. She is the Goddess, and She will be honored, whether in heartfelt love and respect, or in catastrophe. Those who despise her will pay the price.

I say there is now only one way left, one hope for our species: to love Earth. To feel in our hearts that we are a part of Her, what we do to Her we do to ourselves. If you love Earth, you will not fail to evaluate any possible action in light of its effects on the one you love. If you love Earth, then you will vow *earth loyalty*. This is the one way change can come in time: hundreds of millions vow Earth Loyalty. There is no other way.

We are eating the seeds of the future. We are damaging Earth's immune system, her ability to repair damage. This will lead to a fever so severe as to reduce us to at most a minor nuisance, after which recovery will emerge over the next 100 million years or so.

If Mama ain't happy, ain't NOBODY happy!

• • •

Let us have done with the judgment of God! The God who is pure light. The God in whom there is no darkness at all. The God of absolute clarity, who dwells in the domain of "clear and distinct ideas."

The darkness inside the earth is not the place of demons and horror. Rather it is where the seeds sprout and grow. The darkness inside the body is not the source of evils. Rather it is the place where life proliferates and renews itself. Passions of the flesh are not evil; without them the world would cease to turn. That life must end in death is not a mistake of the divine Goddess. "The ways of the Underworld are perfect." Without death, life would be imperfect and one-sided. Nothing fresh or new could ever happen.

Evil comes because people seek to impose an order other than the ecological order of nature. Humans do not accept human ecology, their own place in the scheme of things. The attempt to have light without dark, day without night, spirit without body, life without death—the arrogant wish to conquer and rule all this happening illimitably earth—this is the source of evil.

It is the failure to accept limits set for us by the very nature of things. Must we in our blindness and folly go on forever banging our heads against the rock? So it seems, but in reality a limit now appears on the horizon, that of our own extinction. The attempt to replace nature, to physically change the ultimate conditions of our lives on this planet, is now resulting in destruction on the grandest scale. We have aroused Nemesis, the vengeance of the gods. We have set in motion a vast and implacable machinery, all because we have bought in to an adolescent fantasy. Man says, "I am, and there is no other." Then cometh the End.

The Greeks were well aware that humans are not gods, that when men act with godlike presumption, Nemesis rises in their path. The hero may be glorious, but only for a day. Soon he goes down to dusty death. Soon his great works crumble away and are forgotten.

Hitler set out to found the Thousand Year Reich. One thousand is a perfect number, so what is meant is a kingdom that will last forever. It was revealed to Hitler that the Kingdom of God on earth would be a German kingdom. And so . . . he went down, this German hero, ignominiously committing suicide in the ruined capital of the Reich.

More recently the dream of perfection on earth has gripped the American commercial classes. The neoconservatives say we have reached the End of History. Our system has prevailed against all other contenders. It is now our duty to destroy all remaining opposition and so usher in the glorious fulfillment of human history. The American Dream will be fulfilled, for all people. The conflicts and contradictions of history will end; "democracy" will take root everywhere. This is the most recent form of the dream of human dominance. Humans will remake themselves, and the earth will become a technological paradise where every newborn will be issued a laptop. Marx, Lenin, Hitler, Henry Ford and Dick Cheney all believed this fairy tale. And so, alas, have we all believed it, though we might like to forget about that now.

Since all other life on earth exists only to serve humans and their fantasies, the sixth great extinction, the holocaust of Nature, is not a problem. Indeed, it is but one more evidence of the glory of man. This fool who imagines he can be king of the hill forever, cannot read the handwriting on the wall, cannot see that it is his delusions of grandeur that are the real source of disaster. He imagines that Islam is that source because it is "fatal-

istic"; in other words, it accepts the limits of the human condition coura-
geously instead of acting on ecocidal visions of self-aggrandizement.

The whole world has now accepted consumerism as a way of life. According to this philosophy, the planet is only a stockpile of raw materials needing to be transformed into product. "You can have whatever you
want." "You can be whoever you want to be." These are its slogans.

Have as many children as you want! Express yourself! Without a single
thought for the earth! Without an ounce of recognition that we are utterly dependent creatures, that without air, water, food, we perish. That
we ourselves cannot survive on a conquered planet. We lay waste the body
of our Mother, unwilling to acknowledge that we still need her. We never
outgrow our need for the breasts of the Mother.

There is only one way left now: to accept with humility our place on
this earth and to rein in our insane fantasies of superiority and dominance.
Global Warming is our Nemesis, the just reward of our heroic illusions, our
arrogant species narcissism.

My religion is to love the earth, to ask: Will this action I am about to take
contribute to global warming? If all people do as I am doing, can there be
any hope of Peace with the Earth for our species?

If I continue to fly high above the earth in the ecstasy of my self-exaltation,
surely I have not yet got it. I have not yet recognized that my place is on
earth. I am still caught in dreams that cannot be fulfilled. All too soon we
will stand weeping in the collapsing bunker from which we thought we could
rule. *Homo sapiens über Alles.*

There will be no end of history, only a painful adjustment to the reality
of limits: we are born on earth, our destiny is here, not somewhere beyond
the stars.

• • •

Either the earth is a launching pad or the earth is our home.

Once we have attained to outer space, we will not concern ourselves about
the scorched and damaged condition of the launching pad. It will have served
its one time function: to help us reach our true home—outer space.

But if it is our destiny to remain here on earth, if the earth is our only home, then damaging it as we have done is a sign of insanity.

• • •

The religion of the future will be Earth Loyalty. Religion implies specific obligations. For example, confession once a year, fish on Friday, pray toward Mecca five times a day, circumcision, no abortion.

To pollute the earth, the air, the waters will be a serious sin in the religion of the future. The earth is our Mother and the source of our lives and of all sustenance. To poison the earth is a blasphemy.

Those who vow earth loyalty will renounce air travel except in the gravest exigencies.

Such a vow will also include, for women, the promise to bear no more than one child. Men will be obligated to support women in their decision. In the near future, having a second child will be considered shameful and antisocial because the capacity to feed the world's billions of people will be in steep decline; and also because in our billions we are crowding out the other living beings with whom we share this planet. Without the presence of these others, we cannot be ourselves.

An essential religious practice will be to grow a portion of one's own food. To know personally the truth that food comes from the earth, to have, shall we say, a personal relationship with the Earth, will be the mystical core of Earth Loyalty.

Walking will be another essential practice—"walking in a sacred manner"—that is, with the fullest possible awareness of all our relations within the complex fabric of our local ecology.

In sexual intercourse we experience our profound bodily participation in the body of this earth. We enter for a little while a state of identification with the animals, the others with whom we share this planet—the holy animals who show us the way. In the religion of the future, care of the body and the full development of one's sexual nature will be not just tolerated but encouraged for all who are going on to maturity as human beings.

Here are some other obligatory religious practices: Study the processes of life on earth. Know the plants and birds. Become amateur naturalists, learning the flowers and the stars. Develop a feminized science aiming at humans living well on this earth, accommodating ourselves to the essential conditions, learning our place, human ecology. Learning the earth and learning human go together. Lacking knowledge of our place on earth, we lack knowledge of ourselves. Humans cut off from the earth are not fully themselves.

My religion is to love the earth. My spiritual practices, my sacraments, my life arrangements—all follow from this.

How can I love her if I do not know her?
How can I know her if I do not love her?

Let us fly the flag of Earth Loyalty as a public testimony and witness to our vital and primary love. Let us thus express our conviction that it is earth and our right relation with the earth, that are the Source of Human Good.

• • •

Forgive me, Mama, for I have forgotten You.
I have forgotten that, in relation to You,
I will always be as a little child, for
I will always receive my daily bread from You only.

O Mother of All, there is none like unto You.
O beautiful, white and severe in winter,
O green with the green of the new life in spring,
And deep, rich green in the high summer,
And dark, dark with promise and loss as all things
    go under in fall.

As the wheel turns, Mama, we walk Your holy ways,
Our feet in direct contact with Your sacred body.

Thanks, then . . .
Thanks for this life
with all its sadness and limitations,
    ending in death.

Is it not a participation in the everlasting life of the All?
As we touch the earth, we touch the central mystery,
   the living Source of all things.

We are grateful even for the constancy of
Death, Your rhythmic lover,
Bringer of renewal and
Fresh beginnings,
For aye.

Queen of My Heart

broken earth, damaged earth
black queen of my heart
raped and disrespected
considered as nought
used and thrown away
yet queen even so
queen under the hill
singing the blues
raucous, throaty, powerful

your midwest soils exhausted
mines and wells running out
now they are sucking the
last drops from your pure subterranean reservoirs . . .
fossil waters of the Oglala Aquifer
soon gone . . . all gone

we face into a depleted future

the conquistador within ourselves
the tower of strength

false tower of strength
the safe crust of bias
has collapsed
mama

we are coming home
to you now, nursing our
broken hands and broken hearts . . .
home at last in the arms of our
broken mama
our damaged lover

we'll be singing the blues
together

the fish in your oceans
decimated, mama . . .
no more fish in the Grand Banks

we are your conquerors, babe . . .
we enjoyed you in our way
took our pleasure freely
let the tap run
wide open
partying until dawn

and now it's the morning after
mama, and we know
in our empty hearts that things
will never be the same
again

the age of conquest is over
we must find a new way to be

we are with you now, mama
with you for the first time
beaten and exhausted
just like you, mama
truly together for the first time
and finding in our hearts the
terrible primitive strength
to beat on against the odds
the same strength we
know in you, mama . . .
strength to create
new forms of life out of the
blackened landscape of the burned forest
out of the ashy world of
volcanic island newly emerged

from the sea.

Instead of conquest, accommodation
instead of purity, miscegenation and
hybrid vigor
instead of the sovereign master plan
bricolage
instead of the martial trumpet
calling us to battle
the sadness of the guitar
among the pines

we are discovering our weakness now
mama
among the ruins

we love you, mama
we came forth from your belly

and to you we now return
confessing our need
our dependence

we have nowhere else to go
mama
all our hope is in you

o sacred genital earth
bring us forth again
in new forms as yet
undreamed

---

10 MAY 2009

Petroleum, Mon Amour

In the beginning was Oil
    and Oil was with God
    and Oil *was* God.
All things have been made by Oil
    and without Oil was not anything made that was made.
And still today all things are made
    by Oil.

Every kind of paint and dye
    is made by Oil.
All sorts of fuels and lubricants
    are made by Oil.
The gasket on your refrigerator door
    is made by Oil.
The tubes through which life-saving drugs flow into your veins
    and often the life-saving drugs themselves
    are made by Oil.
The condom which protects you from sexually transmitted disease—
    made by Oil.

The linoleum on your kitchen floor
   is made by Oil.
The vinyl dashboard of your car
   is made by Oil.
The fiber woven into blankets, sweaters, pants, jackets, and rugs—
   the insulation in your sleeping bag—
   all made by Oil.
The fuels which drive the tractors on the farms of America
   come from Oil.
The fertilizers and pesticides which enable
   the enormous productivity of those farms
   come from natural gas and . . . Oil.
Ten calories of fossil fuel energy are required to produce
   one calorie of food energy.
The power which transports your vegetables and fruits
   from California, or Mexico, or Chile
   is the power of our God Oil.
Seven gallons of Oil go into the making of a single tire.
Enormous wealth flows into Wall Street
   from all parts of a worldwide empire
   on a river of Oil so cheap
   that transportation is a negligible part of the cost
   of the Braeburn apple from New Zealand
   you ate for lunch yesterday.

The plastic in your TV and your computer
   derives from Oil.
The wars and police actions and intelligence-gathering operations
   so necessary to keep the New World Order up and running
   depend on Oil.
Our world, our era, is one interconnected whole,
   one immense skein of information
   flowing constantly through fiber optic cables
   made from fiberglass and . . . Oil.

Even the wars we fight to secure our future access to Oil
    themselves squander whole oceans of the Black Gold.
All the intellectual, cultural and psychological inputs
    which are plugged so neatly into each one of us—
    how could they function without Oil?
We modern people with our very interesting problems,
    stresses, addictions, and complexities—
    our sophisticated needs and desires—
    could we even exist without Oil?
Are we not in our very being
    children of Oil?
Now the party has been going on for a long, long time.
We are worried now that our sources may be
    drying up, that our suppliers may soon hold out for a price
    higher than we can afford.
Soon we will be longing for one more long cool injection of Oil.
Soon nostalgia for the lost days of wine and roses
    and the delicious erotic caress of Oil
    will saturate our souls.
For as it was in the beginning, so it will be in the end.
Oil is as God for us.
All things were made by Oil, but
    when Oil hides his face from us . . .
    what then?
We will jump from the rooftops.
We will drown ourselves in the depths of the sea.
We will say to the mountains: *Cover us!*
For without Oil we are undone!
We don't even know who we are without Oil.
We do not see where we can fit in,
    in a world without Oil, for we are
    Oil people. Without Oil we
    are nothing.
The President calls for national sacrifice.

We must all tighten our belts so as to fund
   a new Oil exploration initiative.
Perhaps the fine-toothed comb with which the Oil companies
    have raked over this whole planet
    missed a few spots? Perhaps the teeth were not
   fine enough?
Without Oil we are nothing.
When our father Oil dies,
   will we not lose even our name?
We threw away all the traditions that
   in the past
taught people how to live, how to survive
   on this earth.
Trusting Oil alone for our salvation
   we put aside all the obsolete creeds of the past.
Call the anthropologist!
Ring up the Indians!
Maybe they still remember what we
   have forgotten.
O Oil, do not forsake us!
Do not abandon us!
O woe! *Woe!*
Our God is dead. The one we trusted
   for all good things
   has failed us.
We are undone! Finished!
O woe is me. Please pass the cyanide tablets.
The future has become a blank.
I can't bear to go on without my sexy love thang.
Oil, how could you do this to me?
How could you lose your potency when I am still eager and hot?
O please just pump me one more time, Oil,
   you nasty boy!
Let's do the Jim Jones thing!

Let's pop our pills as we
    come together
    one last time!
O God! It feels so good!
Goodbye, my love.
You were the best.
I guess nothing lasts forever.
Goodbye . . .
Goodbye . . .
Good—

---

22 JUNE 2009

Geo-Politics
and Geo-Religion

Summary:

A worldwide civil religion based on nature philosophy and scientific ideas could be a way out of the trap which the world has become.

Until the last couple of centuries, the Western nations shared a tradition known as "natural law." This was not exactly the same thing as what we now call "the laws of nature." Natural law was a kind of condensation of commonsense notions. For example, There is a natural right to self-defense for anyone who is attacked. Similarly, certain types of property rights were considered normal and natural. Natural law was based on tradition as well as on abstract reasoning. The "just war theory" of Catholic thought grew out of natural law.

All modern and modernizing nations agree on established scientific principles, based on empirical knowledge and reasoning. For example, when building a bridge, Newton's laws apply whether in China, India or the United States. Tribal peoples come out of the forest to seek modern medical care, even as they continue shamanic healing methods back in the village.

Despite this agreement on practical applications of natural laws in the scientific sense, science has not as yet yielded much in the way of common ethical or political norms.

In general, the modern social institution "science" has been built up with massive investment by both governments and private organizations, as well as rich benefactors. This is in many ways our modern religion. Just as the people of the forest hang onto their old ways and beliefs even as their worldview creaks and shifts as they accept Christianity and other novel beliefs — so we too hang onto our religious traditions — Christianity, Judaism, Hinduism, Islam, Buddhism — while we shift a good deal of our weight and our real life choices to a new basis in the scientific worldview.

"Better things for better living through chemistry."

Science: Our Benefactor!

"Progress is our most important product." This means scientific and technical progress, leading to a rising standard of living — which is the payoff. Human life is improved in some way. And on the whole, the real purpose which has driven social investment in the increasingly expensive institutions of science has been the increase of human power over nature, which is thought to lead to an improvement in the human condition. No other society has ever believed that the human condition could be improved. Individuals or specific groups might gain greater wealth and power, but humans as a whole, no.

The results have been impressive: medical miracles (trauma care), air and space travel, more and more powerful weapons of war, great machines carving out valuable resources from nature— , from forest and sea, even from the bowels of the earth — no longer considered taboo and off-limits, as in former times. Vast increases in agricultural productivity. Whole nations lifted up to a middle- class level of material life. Discovery of nature's laws, its hidden order, enables new forms of exploitation and domination, and creates immense wealth for those who are well placed within the modern system. Has all this actually improved the human condition for all and everywhere? Not yet. Not only are many left out, living in poverty; but all must live under the shadow of the Bomb and of ongoing ecological collapse.

There is, however, another side to science. So far I have emphasized the place of science within today's society. In the first few centuries of mod-

ern scientific advance, most discoveries were made by gifted amateurs —
gentlemen or clergy who were practicing science as a hobby or avocation.
What drew these men? Their motives were philosophical, not practical or
financial. And meanwhile, most of the technological advances of the early
modern period were the achievements of gifted tinkerers and inventors
and mechanics whose knowledge of physics and chemistry was limited to
practices, without much theory. Windmills, canals, the power loom, the
first steam engine were the products of their efforts. Accident also played
a role, as in the invention of dynamite and of the process for vulcanizing
rubber, or the discovery of penicillin. Only in the twentieth century did
high theory begin to yield practical results otherwise unattainable. Without Einstein, no Bomb.

The philosophical scientist seeks understanding. "The laws of Nature
and of Nature's God," in Jefferson's phrase, were the object of early scien-
tists. Since God the creator was a rational mind, the architect and design-
er of the cosmos, author of nature, it should be possible to think God's
thoughts after Him as we trace out the inherent structures and patterns
and repetitive processes of the world we live in. Nature is rational, and we
may confirm this through experiment. Alexander Pope wrote: "And God
said, 'Let Newton be!', and all was light." Science is benign, giving support
to religious belief and also eventually practical advantages to us the hairless,
fangless weaklings of nature. So it was thought by the leading people of the
eighteenth century.

But now the plot thickens. One science arose among the many that is
somewhat an orphan, the poor country cousin with little in the way of
spectacular equipment, and a bit of an embarrassment really — because
its methods and perspectives are out of sync with the general program of
science as a great social institution and improver of the human condition.
It is as if this one branch of science were still the province of starry-eyed
amateurs, poetic visionaries seeking knowledge for its own sake rather than
knowledge as a means to human power and advantage. Insight into the
ways of God in the world, perhaps; but promising few immediate payoffs.

I speak of course of ecology, the subversive science, a branch of biology that studies whole life communities, the field of mutual effects and

interconnections of all the life forms in a region or ecological province. Each life-form or species can live only in its own particular niche within the whole living system, although it is also true that living systems are always changing and evolving, and thus no niche is fixed forever. The object of study is this whole living system and its laws. Food chains, population dynamics, who's eating whom, the interdependence and interconnectedness of all living things on the earth, flows of energy and materials through living systems — these things are the subject matter of scientific ecology.

Something ironic happens here, and this is my major point. Whereas physics grants us humans godlike power to destroy life on earth and to visit the moon; whereas chemistry enables us to wipe out or decimate insects that obstruct our purposes; whereas biology enables us to understand the intricacies of cellular life, leading to development of ingenious new medical treatments; ecology says: Go gently, mortals! Be discreet! An antique wisdom. "Humans, know your place! You too are among the animals, and the laws of life impose limits on your dreams of conquest and domination."

Traditional-thought societies sought regulatory principles, considered to be grounded in the very nature of things, in order to restrain the destructive and antisocial side of human potential. International law still to this day is grounded in elementary ideas of fairness and reciprocity and cooperation — as all seek to live in peace on this one earth for reasons of enlightened self-interest. In the past it was assumed by all that we live in a moral universe and that a greater knowledge of nature's laws could actually provide additional support for moral behavior and the peaceful coexistence of peoples.

Instead science led to the development of weapons of mass destruction. Criminal minds gravitate toward the controls of these weapons. Today society as a whole is being turned into a military assemblage. Methods developed to control populations in chaotic war zones are coming back home in the form of sophisticated surveillance systems designed to identify suspicious groups, of possible subversive tendencies. True, you haven't committed a crime; but you might commit one. You are part of a suspect population sector — guilt by association operates freely here.

The hypermasculine military mind lusts for Full Spectrum Dominance, not just of distant battlefields but of all people. Science has gradually become the handmaiden of this dream of total control. Exterminate all useless life! Damaging insects! Plants that have no use in our society. Wild and uncontrolled landscapes which serve no purpose save the need for natural beauty cultivated by a small and privileged cultural elite. And people too, those identified by Henry Kissinger as "useless eaters." Those who serve neither as consumers nor as producers . . . are standing in the way of progress. Our own minds are being taken over, drafted into service as the most terrible weapons of all. Drive an SUV and be safe from the others, the dark horde that populate the feral core of the world's cities, including even those here at home. Make sure you end up on the side of the controllers and their lethal technologies, not among the useless masses of the controlled. Better predator than prey is increasingly the maxim of our time.

Ecology stands unperturbed by these horrific developments. Ecology says: "Continue in the direction you are going, and you will get to where you are headed." Your dreams of total control will not be fulfilled. Full Spectrum Dominance will not be achieved. In the very nature of things you will pay the price of your delusions of grandeur. Rein in your fantasies! Trim your sails before you fall into an abyss from which there will be no exit. You, Man, are violating the laws of Nature and of Nature's God, and so entering into a tragic and unavoidable destiny — unless you repent. Unless you change your way of thinking. Unless you undergo a radical renewal of your minds . . ."

Thus saith the Lord: Thus far and no farther shall you go! That is, the Lord Science. No one, as far as I know, denies that ecology is a genuine science. In addition there is the second law of thermodynamics, which says that after you have burned the oil, there is no way to reverse the process and get it back. Science says NO to endless growth. It ain't going to happen. Once you've used it up, it's gone forever. There are also the findings of climate science, which could be viewed as an extension of ecology on a world scale.

One worldwide interconnected weather system, immensely complex and beyond our control, and moving in a direction that will prove hazardous to us paragons of creation.

Science not as a means of domination but as a way to understand how things are, offers in my opinion a possible basis for understanding among peoples, peace, and cooperation. What I call Earth Loyalty means passionate adherence to a way of life grounded in actual knowledge of the earth, of the life processes which are the only possible basis of our continuation as a species on this planet. The various fundamentalisms lead only to partisan idolatries and vainglorious war.

We require a universal view. Science has provided a basis for fundamental agreements if we care to use it in that way. We are all together here on this one earth, which is our only home. The only way out of our predicament is to turn back to the earth and submit to its laws.

The very word *Islam* means submission. We may find this disgusting and backward, but all spiritual traditions include an element of submission — one must bow to the greater powers, however they are conceived and imagined. This does not go down well with the Man of the Modern Age, who imagines that he is the culmination and pinnacle of all human history and culture to date.

The wise voices of the ages say: Man, you are too elated. You are bloated with a false and empty imagining of your place. Cast away these barren dreams and know your place. Discover the truth about where you fit it.

At the present time the Western virus has spread to the whole world. China now leads the charge toward infinite growth in a finite world. The oldest continuous culture on earth — in which ideas of balance and of humans as a part of nature came to elegant expression — has thrown its own tradition overboard and is now joining us in the mad project of burning the ship in order to fuel the massive blast needed for lift-off, as we slip the surly bonds of earth and lose our senses altogether.

Let people maintain their religions and traditions as they will, while at the same time agreeing that Earth Loyalty must be the binding obligation upon us all. Let Earth Loyalty function in today's situation as natural law did in the past — a way we can all work together toward common understandings of the human condition in our time, the necessities imposed on all by the very nature of things. Let them all work out ways to reconcile this notion with their traditions, so that Earth Loyalty will appear simply as the expression of traditional insight in a form appropriate to the era we are now entering. Just as in the U.S. we have had a civil religion which binds us into a provisional and workable unity, while at the same time we espouse a wide variety of churches and sects; so let Earth Loyalty become the civil religion of all people everywhere, even as they continue their various religious traditions, modifying and adapting them as seems appropriate to them.

The age of Earth Domination is over. It is finished. The age of Earth Loyalty is beginning, grounded in the new/old understanding of the laws of nature and of nature's god, which may be found in the science and worldview of ecology.

2010

The Self-Provisioning Community[3]

WE HUMANS WILL either acknowledge that we are a part of the earth, or we will continue to move toward our own extinction. Consciousness of our participation in the earth's dynamic life processes cannot emerge so long as our everyday lives continue to be ordered by the rituals of domination.

For five hundred years and more we humans have been moving away from the practices of self-provisioning; from obtaining our livelihoods directly from our own places and from the natural productive life of the earth, and toward consumerism. Instead of getting our food and clothing and housing from the land under hand and foot, or from the nearby woods, or from the sea, we obtain what we need through the distancing media of advertising, long-distance transport, impersonal private syndicates, prison-like factories, and money. Everything in our economic lives tells us: You don't really belong here. You are separate and apart from the earth and the creatures of the earth. You are part of a World System which is the Lord and Dominator and Decider of the fate of all the earth.

---

[3] Talk presented to the New Haven–Quinnipiac Bioregional Group and Transition Greater New Haven, December 6, 2010

Originally published in *Planet Drum Pulse* (Spring 2011)

Our relation to earth is one of mining, extraction, total objectification. At the present time we are engaged in a great collective project of asset stripping. Time spent away from everyday rituals — in wilderness — may restore a sense of being here as a part of the earth — but only partially and only temporarily. Soon we return to our usual routines, which reinforce the identity of an industrial person in an age of nihilism, for whom anything goes; and we ourselves become but products of the Modern World System.

Since we no longer touch and realize the earth as a self-sufficient living system, it is very difficult to sense our own dependence on that system. As "normal modern people" we almost inevitably and unconsciously transfer our loyalty and feeling of dependence to the Modern World System. It would seem, in practice, that there is no alternative. Those who still try to "get in touch with Mother Earth" are romantic, backward-looking. In today's usage, the word "romantic" has become a pejorative.

But our loyalty to the World System is a suicide pact, a covenant of death for our species.

There is a way to move against this frightening monster, which has such a terrific life of its own. We can begin to move toward self-provisioning. We need not envision moving all the way back to, say, the Middle Ages . . . or even farther back, to hunter-gatherer ways. All that is necessary is to change direction. Our present way of life is like someone adding each day one more brick to the prison we have all been building unconsciously. In contrast, we could remove one brick each day. It is our daily practices which we take for granted and perform automatically that are these bricks. We can begin, little by little, to change our practices. To become sustainable we must transform our economy into many local economies. We must shorten our lines of supply and reduce our dependence on nonrenewable fuels, by relocalizing.

Living in place has its disciplines and tasks, its practices. On the day that you take a shovel and, with your own hands, dig up a piece of ground to plant a vegetable garden — you are moving toward self-provisioning; hence moving against the stream of "totalizing" commerce and technology. On the day that you begin to build a pantry, taking back from the corporations the task of providing for yourself and your loved ones or buddies — you are moving toward self-provisioning. On the day when you begin to think and work deliberately to increase your own and your community's emergency preparedness, no longer believing that one of Big Brother's little helpers will take care of you if something happens — you are already moving toward self-provisioning.

It is time to unplug, time to withdraw our faith from the World System upon which we have been and remain so shamefully dependent. This system is unstable and unreliable. Lose your faith in Progress! Progress is destroying the earth as a fit habitat for humans.

But how can we turn again to the earth in an authentic way? Spending your vacation in a "natural area" is not enough. We must change our lives, beginning now. We must establish dissenting practices, weave them firmly into the very fabric of our everyday lives. This is the only way for us to move toward a sustainable society. One by one we withdraw our faith from the present all-encompassing and (only) seemingly irresistible World System, placing our trust instead in the living earth, and expressing this trust in specific and necessarily local ways. Bioregionalism is a Way, an ensemble of practices which will be essential to the emergence of a sustainable society. There can be no sustainability without it.

We are interested in native peoples because they take for granted the meaningfulness of being a participant in the community of life on earth in their place. Each place stimulates and supports the evolution of a distinctive cultural assemblage appropriate to that place. The place itself teaches bioregional values and practices, if only we pay attention. Renewal of subsistence practices will be the way in which we humans will ultimately be restored to the status of participants in the great life, and delivered from the hell of separate and meaningless existence.

Archaic societies have in common the belief that the earth is enough. None see the earth as essentially threadbare and worthless and thus requiring that we build unnatural and/or otherworldly palaces to assuage our hungering hearts. Earth is alive, generating ever-new forms. To align with the earth is not to move toward stasis and sterile repetition; rather it implies energy to imagine and generate new arrangements.

I cannot enter into a caring and committed relationship with the earth as a whole; rather, I must express my care and commitment in a place. I must stay put long enough to know my place in detail and to align my own life with the life of my place. Only thus do I have a chance to reweave the body and soul connection with "all my relations." The proper unit of survival is the local community. The grandeur of empire is a sham. When push comes to shove, the empire will not be there for us; it will use us for its own purposes. (Remember Hurricane Katrina.)

We need practices that tie us into the web of life in our place. Otherwise we will be no more than alienated drifters on this earth. These practices must also build gradually the local community of reinhabitants. "All our relations" must include our relations with each other within a place-based human community, that is, a community which includes all the people who live here and offers all the chance to participate in the creative process of inventing this new, local, sustainable way of life. (A sustainable local community will continue to trade and interact with other places. It will not be isolated, but it will produce as much as possible of its own basic necessities.)

As the Zen practitioner rises every day, sips some tea, and then sits in meditation for half an hour, we bioregionalists must needs walk. Without this practice we wouldn't know who we are. Apart from walking, how could we know where we are? This body is passing through this landscape as it is, scarred by human abuse, covered by infrastructure, yet still alive. Bioregionalism begins with a soul connection to the land itself, to the actual earth of value in a particular place.

Together we walk the watersheds of our life-place. With our feet we establish contact with the larger system of earthly life which predates the industrial age and which will remain after that age lies in ruins. With our hands we reach out and establish contact with each other, connecting into the human community as but a part of the larger community of life. Walking together is a vital practice of those who are moving toward sustainability. It is through our horizontal links with others — the animal people, the human people, and the tree people — that we recover a knowledge of who we are and can be: dwellers in the earth.

Eating together is another such practice. Sharing the fellowship of earthly life, eating the fruits of our local earth and also gifts of food from nearby woods, lakes, streams, and sea; we recognize that we are part of complex food chains. Across the table we look into each others' eyes and say, "Partaking in this food we acknowledge that we too are participants in the earth. Together we are walking toward a greater and richer awareness of all our relations. There is no separation."

Growing food is also a key component of relocalizing our lives. To obtain a yield from the actual ground where we live is an obligation of the Bioregional Way. Even for apartment dwellers, there are ways to do this: community gardens, a friend's yard, or a container on the balcony. It is also possible to obtain a yield from our local region through foraging, fishing, or hunting.

When I connect to the Earth System by eating local food and food I have helped to grow myself, whether in a home garden or in a communally cultivated garden, or wild food I have collected, I also disconnect from the arrogant system of earth domination of which the supermarket is but one expression. When I consciously taste and drink the water of my own watershed, I bring the industrial water suppliers down a notch. They are only distributing what the earth and the great weather freely gave. All water is ultimately wild water. None of it was made in a factory.

Every practice which tends to remove the layers of mediating systems and institutions and structures between me and the Earth System is a practice of life instead of death for our species. Each practice has both a material and a spiritual or mental pole. The food I grow in my garden is real food, which really and truly sustains my body. That food also serves as a symbolic expression of my relation with the earth. For the bioregionalist, every meal truly is a sacramental meal, and every potluck deepens our soul connection to both place and community.

Many other practices we can embrace today, as we transition toward a low-energy future, fall under the heading of local production for local use. We can initiate small-scale local manufacturing, preparing for the time when China will no longer supply our stuff. We can recycle materials from deconstructed buildings. We can share skills — subsistence practices —for self-provisioning with those who want to learn. We can engage in barter, and in complex systems of barter. We can make clothing or recycle clothing. We can work to establish reasonable practices of emergency preparedness. We can keep warm or cool mostly by adapting and improving our present housing stock. We can increase the usability of housing by living together with more people in each house. We can work out new ways of developing group coherence and living at peace in closer quarters and more intense ways of mutual dependence. We can foster groups as natural units of survival, against the stream of consumerist individualism. Finally, we can work together collectively to change the rules of the social-political-economic game to make them more supportive of our values; but this can only happen after enough people have actually begun to change their own lives, and when specific openings appear.

If, as many of us sense, we are living at a time of crisis, leading up to a big change — "the end of the world as we know it," in Immanuel Wallerstein's phrase — the slow crumbling or fast collapse of the World System; then the most vital question for us today must be: What can we do now that will continue to sustain us on the other side of history? We can establish practices of self-provisioning which will continue to function as part of daily habits under changed conditions. Growing food, storing food, walking together, eating together (all with awareness) will go with us as we pass, as it were, through the sound barrier in reverse, and into a new era.

We have no blueprint of that era. The whole pattern cannot be known except through ongoing processes of creative change as things unfold. Humans at home on Earth will imagine new blossomings again and again. But we can take up practices that already, in the present, express our changed relation with the earthly sources of our lives, and provide continuity as we come into a time when such practices will necessarily become widespread. We can take up practices that 1) express our disaffection from the present set-up, 2) reconnect us to the earth life now, and 3) reward us already in this present time with satisfactions that will feed our souls and give us heart and courage to continue in the face of vast carnage. Without this soul connection, we will not have the fortitude to carry on, nor will it be possible to enter fully into a new knowledge of ourselves as dwellers and participants in the earth.

There is no alternative.

Have you lost your faith in Progress? Are you practicing at the present time the rites of participation in the community of life in your place? Are you moving toward self-provisioning, taking small steps on that path through specific practices? Are you obtaining a yield? Have you changed your life?

Each one teach one.

---

6 DECEMBER 2010

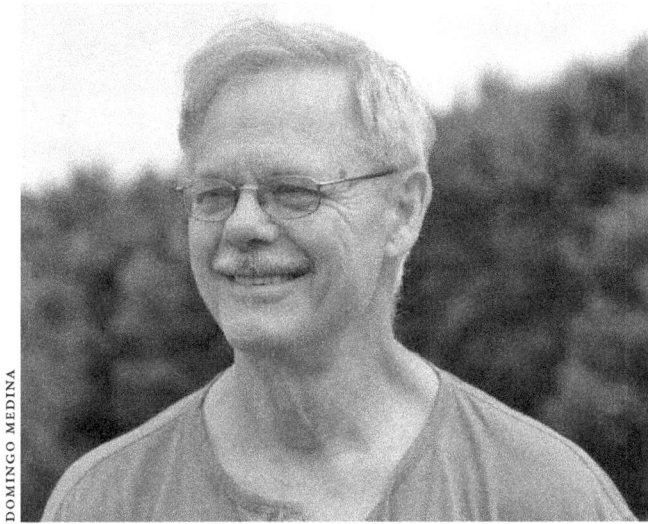

DOMINGO MEDINA

ABOUT THE AUTHOR

Fred Cervin was an environmental activist, a bioregionalist, a philosopher, and a poet. He presented his ideas on earth-based spirituality and the future of human society through a series of stirring talks and poetry readings in his local New Haven, Connecticut, community. To put his ideas into action, he cofounded the New Haven Bioregional Group in 2005. Fred died of complications from cancer in August of 2013. The following biographical note was found among his writings.

Fred Cervin — Brief Biography

Fred (Frederick R.) Cervin, b. 1940. Grew up Chicago, Seattle, Sioux City. Minnesota lakes. Evangelical background, minister father. 1956: biology class a revelation; hiked Grand Canyon; Garden of the Gods by moonlight. Whitman. Studied philosophy in college; had psychotherapy. Jung. Whitehead. 1970: seminary degree. Homesteaded in Maine 1970–73. Pastor 1973–78. Withdrew from Church 1979. Took up carpentry. Divorced 1983. Lived alone for ten years. Began intense study of poetry; began writing. Dream work. Continued working as carpenter.

1988: settled in New Haven. Continued studies: bioregionalism, Deep Ecology, Deleuze and Guattari, Gary Snyder, Paul Shepard. 1994: Moved in with Maria Tupper. 1998: Deep Ecology Workshop, Aspen. Wrote more poetry, songs, essays. Nietzsche studies. Robinson Jeffers, Charles Olson. Occasional poetry readings. 2001: diagnosed with Waldenstrom's macroglobulinemia (a rare lymphoma); treated successfully. 2005: played leading role in organizing one-day Peter Berg conference. Cofounded New Haven Bioregional Group. Heinberg, Kunstler, Ruppert, Jensen. 2006: Maria Tupper joins Bioregional Committee. Walks, movies, potlucks. 2007: Bioregional Garden begins; *What a Way to Go* showing draws audience of 80. Fred retires from carpentry. 2008: Bioregional Mapping Group. July 1, 2008: second major round of chemotherapy concludes successfully.

Plans: Continue bioregional work. Make a book of my writings. Breathe deeply. Let go. Love the Earth.